ANIMALS AROUND THE WORLD

ALL ABOUT ASIAN

BENGAL TIGERS

Carol Kline

Creating Young Nonfiction Readers

EZ Readers lets children delve into nonfiction at beginning reading levels. Young readers are introduced to new concepts, facts, ideas, and vocabulary.

Tips for Reading Nonfiction with Beginning Readers

Talk about Nonfiction
Begin by explaining that nonfiction books give us information that is true. The book will be organized around a specific topic or idea, and we may learn new facts through reading.

Look at the Parts
Most nonfiction books have helpful features. Our *EZ Readers* include a Contents page, an index, and color photographs. Share the purpose of these features with your reader.

Contents
Located at the front of a book, the Contents displays a list of the big ideas within the book and where to find them.

Index
An index is an alphabetical list of topics and the page numbers where they are found.

Photos/Charts
A lot of information can be found by "reading" the charts and photos found within nonfiction text. Help your reader learn more about the different ways information can be displayed.

With a little help and guidance about reading nonfiction, you can feel good about introducing a young reader to the world of *EZ Readers* nonfiction books.

Mitchell Lane

PUBLISHERS

2001 SW 31st Avenue
Hallandale, FL 33009
www.mitchelllane.com

First Edition, 2020.

Author: Carol Kline
Designer: Ed Morgan
Editor: Sharon F. Doorasamy

Names/credits:
Title: All About Asian Bengal Tigers / by Carol Kline
Description: Hallandale, FL :
Mitchell Lane Publishers, [2020]

Series: Animals Around the World
Library bound ISBN: 9781680204025
eBook ISBN: 9781680204032

EZ readers is an imprint of Mitchell Lane Publishers

Library of Congress Cataloging-in-Publication Data
Names: Kline, Carol, 1957- author.
Title: All about Asian bengal tigers / by Carol Kline.
Description: First edition. | Hallandale, FL : EZ readers, an imprint of Mitchell Lane Publishers, 2020. | Series: Animals around the world-Asian animals | Includes bibliographical references and index.
Identifiers: LCCN 2018032700| ISBN 9781680204025 (library bound) | ISBN 9781680204032 (ebook)
Subjects: LCSH: Bengal tiger—Juvenile literature.
Classification: LCC QL737.C23 K594 2020 | DDC 599.756—dc23
LC record available at https://lccn.loc.gov/2018032700

Photo credits: Freepik.com, Shutterstock, mapchart.net

3 5944 00143 5617

CONTENTS

Bengal Tigers   4

Where Do Bengal Tigers Live?   22

Interesting Facts   23

Parts of a Bengal Tiger   23

Glossary   24

Further Reading   24

On the Internet   24

Index   24

Bengal tigers are the largest of all cats. They live in India. Tigers are known for their **strength**.

Bengal tigers are orange with brown or black stripes. The tiger's belly is white. The tail is orange with black rings.

The stripes are different on every tiger. The stripes help them to hide.

8

9

A tiger is as big as a pony. Its paws are as big as a dinner plate.

11

Bengal tigers eat meat. They hunt deer and water buffalo. They eat rabbits and porcupines too.

Tigers hunt at night. They **pounce**. They strike with their claws. They bite on the neck too.

Female tigers give birth to one to five **cubs** at a time. They raise their cubs alone. Cubs start to hunt during their first year.

Tigers hide from people. **Hunters** kill tigers for their skin, bones, and teeth. They sell their claws too.

19

People cut down the **forests** where tigers live. This makes it hard for them. India has created special places to help tigers live in the wild.

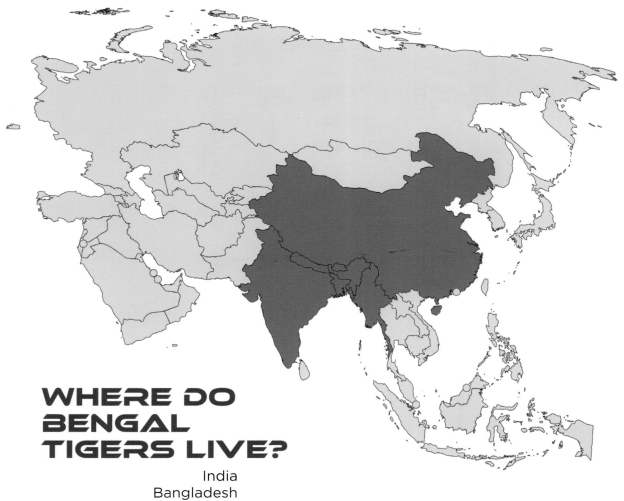

WHERE DO BENGAL TIGERS LIVE?

India
Bangladesh
Nepal
Bhutan
China
Myanmar

INTERESTING FACTS

- Tigers live 8 to 10 years in the wild.

- Tigers are important to Indian **tradition** and **culture**.

- Tigers can jump up to 33 feet. That is five times the height of a person.

- Bengal Tigers are featured on a postage stamp sometimes called the "Tiger Stamp." Buying the stamp provides money to help tigers.

PARTS OF A BENGAL TIGER

Claws
The claws of a tiger can retract into its paws, just like a cat.

Stripes
Each tiger has unique stripes, which means they are not like any other tiger's. The stripes are brown or black. The rest of the tiger's fur is orange to white.

Teeth
A tiger's teeth can grow to be three inches long. This is as long as an adult's finger.

Belly
The skin on a tiger's belly is loose.

Tail
A tiger's tail is two to 3.5 feet long.

GLOSSARY

cub
Baby tiger

culture
The habits or beliefs of a group of people

forest
A large area of trees

hunter
A person who hunts wild animals

pounce
To attack suddenly

strength
The quality of being strong

tradition
A way of behaving that has continued for a long time

FURTHER READING

Peterson, Megan Cooley. *Bengal Tigers are Awesome!* North Mankato, MN: Capstone Press, 2016.

Spilsbury, Louise, and Richard Spilsbury. *Bengal Tiger.* Chicago, Il: Heinemann Library, 2006.

ON THE INTERNET

Visit Bengal tigers at the San Diego Zoo in California at this online site which features links to tiger sounds, such as a roar and a snarl
http://animals.sandiegozoo.org/animals/tiger

Tigers for Kids: Learn All About Tigers—FreeSchool
https://www.youtube.com/watch?v=jEQaRY4YpVo

INDEX

Claws   15, 19, 23
India   4, 20, 22
Hunter   19
Stripes   7, 8, 23
Tiger Stamp 23